Escape from Latvia:
My Father's Diary

By Ingrid McGowan, DM

Escape from Latvia: My Father's Diary

Ingrid McGowan, DM

Table of Contents

Preface

On September 7, 1944, my father, Nikolajs Leonids Garais and his wife of five months, Erika, escaped from their homeland of Latvia to start a voyage to a new life.

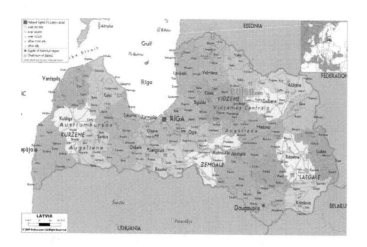

Political Map of Latvia

ezilon.com

The Soviets had invaded Latvia, first in 1940, then returning in 1944 after the 1941 German occupation to consume the small country to the point where life became intolerable and dangerous for its citizens. Most of them were descended from Latvians who lived through centuries of being occupied; now many were escaping the violence by any means possible and heading for asylum in Germany, Austria, Scandinavia, South America and even Australia. Not knowing if they would ever return to Latvia, Nikolajs and Erika boarded a Belgian cargo ship in Riga along with others seeking refuge in Germany.

The Belgian cargo ship Moero[1]

---

[1] www.wrecksite.eu

Escape from Latvia: My Father's Diary

Ironically, just two weeks after Nikolajs and Erika debarked, the Moero was sunk during an air raid on September 22, 1944.

The following is a loosely translated English version of the diary Nikolajs started the day they left. I have taken liberties with the translation, because I have no reference besides the journal itself other than increasingly vague memories of hearing my parents talk about Germany. Some words are hard to read, having been written in pencil and having survived the 73 years since the journal was started. Many terms are technical, specific to war, and most likely would have been used by someone with personal experience with aircraft and wartime, as Nikolajs had. Latvians were recruited into German military service during the occupation and Nikolajs worked, as many did, in an aircraft factory.

The diary surfaced after Nikolajs died in May 1994. He had never spoken of it that I could remember, so it was a shocking discovery. My first few attempts at translation came up against metaphoric brick walls that arose when I felt the emotion of Erika's sadness or Nikolajs' sarcasm, or when it was just too much to try and translate some of the difficult terminology. I overcame these obstacles and, with the help of an older Latvian-English dictionary provided by a relative, I was able to interpret most of the language as it was in the 1940s.

Included in the translation are numerous annotations to explain what I perceive to have been true, but I apologize to my parents' souls if I have misrepresented words or intentions. In a few cases, I was unable to find translations for particular words and have so indicated.

Nikolajs' and Erika's experiences were very real, and are symbolic of what has happened to political refugees throughout the millennia. While this account is brief, it provides dramatic insight into the lives of displaced persons (DPs) in Germany near the end of World War II. As much as possible, I have inserted historical or geographic references, photographs, or maps to support and clarify the details of the journey. The introduction is intended to lay a foundation for who Erika and Nikolajs were, according to the limited information I gleaned from them while growing up. Following the translation is a compilation of experiences and thoughts about our family relationships that will offer readers a glimpse of who Erika and Nikolajs became.

Escape from Latvia: My Father's Diary

During my research, I came across a wonderful book entitled "Memoirs of Childhood in DP Camps in Germany" by Karlis Dankers. I contacted him through social media and requested permission to add his work as a reference. His account of his family's experiences gave me insight as to how I might structure this book and I will always be grateful that he wrote his memoirs before I attempted to put this together.

I have also read Ruth Sepetys', "Between Shades of Grey", that chronicles the lives of Lithuanians captured by the Soviets and exiled to Siberia in 1941. Although Nikolajs and Erika's experiences were not as dire as those lived by Sepetys' family, this account, nevertheless, has similarities in how many Baltic exiles must have felt during that time.

Also offering background knowledge to my writing is Dagnija Neimane's, "Flight from Latvia, A Six-Year Chronicle". In it, the author provides a historical and social context for her family's experiences as they, too, escaped the Soviet invasion. Her perspectives include details of military movements and other events of which no mention is made in Nikolajs' diary. These differences underscore how personal each individual's experiences were.

The translation of the diary is introduced with chapters containing whatever information I have about Erika and Nikolajs' early years leading up to their departure from Latvia in 1944. Many of the photographs are undated, but they tell part of the story and provide poignant illustrations of their early lives. Most of the photographs are part of a collection inherited from my parents. Others are annotated with sources.

The diary spans a short period of time from the departure date to early 1946. The experiences detailed in the journal lay the foundation for the people Erika and Nikolajs became and how their lives developed. The trauma of living through the escape most probably contributed to their early demise due to illnesses that may have been caused by the unimaginable stress of war. Erika was only 70 when she died in 1992 of breast and ovarian cancer, while Nikolajs lasted only two years longer.

Writing this account was an intensely emotional experience for me. I learned a great deal about my parents, our family dynamics, and myself. It is with great pleasure that I share the results of my efforts. I hope you gain satisfaction from reading the book and please know how much I appreciate your interest.

*   *   *

Chapter I --- Erika

Erika Garais (née Jakobsons) was born on August 3, 1921 to Liza (Krums) and Johans Teodors Jakobsons in the town of Valmiera in Vidzeme's province, Latvia. Her family home was located in Limbaži.

Brother Janis, mother Lizu, Erika ca. 1925

Uncle and Aunt (names unknown), sister Erna, mother Liza, Erika, father Johans , ca. 1927

The story of the family, as related to me by my cousin, Ruta, (daughter of Erika's older sister, Erna) was that Erika's mother, Liza, was already wealthy from having inherited the large estate of her parents, who were banished to Siberia at some point under early Communist rule. Liza was left to manage the family business until she married Johans, about 15 years her junior. Even by modern standards, she was an unusually accomplished woman who achieved professional success and also typified the strong matriarchal figure representative of Latvian society.

Erika was the youngest of three children, with brother, Janis, the oldest, born in 1914, and sister, Erna, born in 1919. According to my mother's recounting, the family was wealthy and maintained a large grain growing business. They had servants and Erika is unlikely to have wanted for anything material while she was growing up. Although their home was technically a farm, Erika and her siblings did not have to participate in its operation.

I always considered her a bit of a princess, and the family lineage apparently did contain some aristocracy, although this was never researched or confirmed. I remember references to Prussian and Estonian in her background, but ethnic pride would prevent any serious acknowledgement of anything that would dilute a true Latvian ancestry.

The following photograph is of Erika's fifth grade class and, coincidentally, also contains a classmate whose daughter ended up becoming my best friend in Montreal many years later.

Erika's fifth grade class picture – third from left second row

Erika was a girl guide[2] in her early teens and she later attended high school in Bauska. From her own admission, she was not an exceptional student and may or may not have attended university if the war had not interrupted her youth. In Europe, higher education is based on aptitude and achievement in lower grades, so she may not have had the ability to

---

[2] The British/European/Canadian equivalent of Girl Scouts.

attain the necessary standards for college entrance. Through-out her life, Erika was sociable and enjoyed being around peo-ple.

Erika is seated at the far right of the center row — the Guides appear to be demonstrating needlework.

Erika was the youngest in the family and, most likely, was spoiled by her parents and siblings. She spoke of her childhood in positive terms, seemingly didn't lack for anything, and was well cared for by her mother as well as by the servants employed on the large farm.

Sister Erna and Erika on July 30, 1939 in Limbaži

Erika, brother Janis and sister Erna ca. 1939

Erika idolized her oldest brother, Janis, and never again being able to see him after leaving Latvia must have been devastating. Janis spent several years in Soviet prison camps in the

1950s as punishment for his participation in the Germany military service, which Latvian men were required to do under German occupation. He was released and returned to his home around 1960 to spend his final years in poor health, but alive.

Janis October 1960

According to Erika, Janis' life before the incarceration was somewhat wild, full of drinking and motorcycle riding. After he returned from Siberia, he lost his leg in a motorcycle accident. He and his wife had one daughter, Ilze, with whom I have connected on social media and whose children resemble mine.

Erika's sister Erna date ca. 1910

Erika's sister, Erna, whom I had the opportunity to meet when she visited my parents in Montreal in 1989, had a very different personality from Erika's. Of course, by then, the sisters were most likely so happy to be able to be together, whatever personality differences may have existed as children no longer caused them any discord. Erna died in 2004 from heart failure. Her daughter, Ruta, visited us in 2007 and two of her daughters have been here recently to visit us. As I write this, Ruta is planning a trip to Florida in November 2017, so we will once again be able to spend time together and share memories of our respective mothers.

Erika ca. 1943

Erika's early sunshiny nature was, no doubt, tarnished throughout the years by the misery she felt being away from her home and family. One early notation in the diary (p. 46, footnote 24) alludes to her cheerful disposition, but my impression of her growing up saw the optimism eventually dissipate into bitterness and cynicism. Interestingly enough, while researching translation, I came upon the realization that, although my Latvian vocabulary is quite well developed, never had my family used the word for "enjoy". Thinking back, this does not surprise me, especially regarding Erika.

* * *

Chapter II - Nikolajs

Nikolajs Leonids Garais was born on December 9, 1917 in Riga, Latvia. Nikolajs was a self-acclaimed city boy and, in my childhood, would tell stories of catching rides on the backs of streetcars in the city streets. He was an avid athlete and practiced sports until he was no longer able to in the last few years of his life. He played volleyball, basketball, cycled on racing bikes, ice skated, and cross-country skied at a pre-olympic level. He probably would have qualified for the Olympics had the war not come along.

Nikolajs (second from left front row) with basketball team

His love of sports was adversely affected by marriage, since Erika did not share his passion, nor did he have a son in whom he could instill the same. Fortunately for Nikolajs, I was born with an interest in sports, although my mother made sure my activities were limited to ballet and the occasional recreational volleyball game. Ladies simply did not do sports.

Nikolajs ca. 1940

Nikolajs was a talented artist, although it is unclear when he began to practice these talents that, later in life, contributed to his legacy of beautiful oil paintings and sketches.

His military service under German occupation led to employment as a draftsman and, later in life, to his profession as a commercial artist. Nikolajs lacked the confidence to rely on his painting and drawing talent for income, although, with the right marketing, his works probably could have made him famous.

Nikolajs' parents, Emma and Edvards Garais date unknown

Of Nikolajs' family not much is known aside from his father's name, Edvards Garais, and his mother's name, Emma Garais (née Kreilis). Although the family lived in the heart of the city, their property was large enough to permit their own beekeeping and Nikolajs was a lifelong lover of honey.

His parents must have experienced overwhelming loneliness after the departure of their son and subsequent death of their daughter, Velta (see p. 16). They raised Velta's son, Andrejs, and somehow managed to endure the effects of the war on their lives. Nikolajs' mother lived well into her nineties.

The Garais family home on Dzutes street was occupied by the Soviets, most likely during the invasion of 1944, but eventually his parents must have been able to return to it. A letter was mailed by his nephew, Andrejs, to Nikolajs with the return address of the same house on Dzutes street in which Andrejs was living. The postmark is difficult to read, but the letter inside the envelope is dated 1972 and another similar missive is dated 1973. The house was eventually razed and the location is now occupied, ironically, by a sports arena.

Nikolajs' mother in 1965

Envelope from nephew Andrejs at 7 Dzutes Street 1972

Nikolajs' sister Velta ca. 1940s

Nikolajs' sister, Velta, was the older of the two siblings, though by how much it is unclear. She married and had the one son, Andrejs, who maintained contact with Nikolajs until sometime in the late 1980s. Velta suffered from lung disease and died sometime in 1948 or 1949. The legend of her illness as Nikolajs told it to us maintained that she once contracted pneumonia after skiing and subsequently died, but entries in the diary tell a different story. They allude to a chronic lung condition exacerbated by lack of oxygen in an air raid shelter during an enemy attack. It is possible that Nikolajs simply did not want to relive the horror by telling us the truth. After Velta's death, Andrejs was cared for by Nikolajs' parents and his eventual marriage resulted in the birth of daughters, including a set of twins.

Due to the preponderance of daughters in the family, the Garais surname was lost as related to this particular unit. Nikolajs did speak of twin uncles, Nikolajs and Leonids (hence, his name), and research shows the existence of people named Garais in Latvia as well as in parts of Europe, the United States and South America.[3] The twin uncles and twin daughters to Nikolajs' nephew were likely genetic predecessors to the twin boys I bore in 1977.

*   *   *

---

[3] http://www.Namespedia.com/details/Garais

Chapter III – Erika and Nikolajs

Erika and Nikolajs most probably met through mutual friends in a social situation or possibly through colleagues at Espenlaube, the aircraft factory in Riga where evidence shows they both worked. Erika appears in photographs with "Espenlaube" as a notation and Nikolajs received a letter dated October 3, 1944 from his mother addressed to Espenlaube in Germany. This last fact was the clue that Latvian emigrants traveled under the auspices of the factories for which they worked.

Erika (on the left) and colleagues – Espenlaube – early 1940s

Letter to Nikolajs from his mother dated October 3, 1944 addressed to "Espenlaub Flugzeubau in Wuppertal Langerfeld[4]"

If my memories are correct, my parents met through a friend of Erika's in whom Nikolajs was interested, but the details were never very clear. As with much of their past, specifics of their courtship were not often discussed, so I can only imagine the volatile relationship between their distinctly different personalities. Erika and Nikolajs married on April 9, 1944.

---

[4] http://www.gracesguide.co.uk/Espenlaub-Flugzeugbau

Erika and Nikolajs' Wedding Day, April 9, 1944

The wedding could not have been lavish, as is evidenced by their simple attire. They wore simple gold wedding bands that, unfortunately, were "lost" from the baggage that eventually found its way to them in Germany. Throughout the

33

years, neither Erika nor Nikolajs spoke much of the wedding. Even their anniversary was understated and I only remember acknowledging it in their later years.

To this day, I wonder what led to the mutual attraction that impelled them to marry. Erika was a somewhat spoiled, probably immature young lady from a wealthy family living in the country. Nikolajs was rumored to be an urban playboy who continued to flirt into his later life. He was an athlete, which Erika hated, and he loved life in the big city. As the diary unfolds, it is clear that Nikolajs was unprepared to continue some of the pampering Erika expected, and she, on the other hand, was not used to his introverted, artistic personality or sophisticated tastes.

The brief glimpse into Erika and Nikolajs' lives offered by the diary is more than a recounting of the frightening events of late 1944 in war-torn Germany. It is a window into the personalities of two young Latvians who survived that time and many other years to become parents, move several times again, and somehow, stay together in spite of not being particularly compatible in the first place. The diary also adds to the growing body of knowledge about "displaced persons", or DPs, as these refugees were designated. Much of WWII history focuses

Escape from Latvia: My Father's Diary

on the Holocaust, but little has been done to unearth the experiences of non-Jewish DPs like Erika and Nikolajs.

* * *

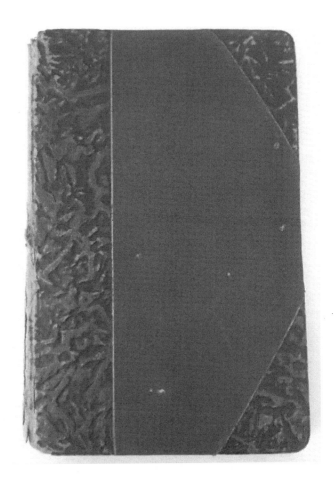

A photo of the actual diary

Chapter IV --- The Diary

The opening page of the diary.

September 7, 1944

We're on the ship. Nothing else to do – we have to go.
It was so hard leaving Mamiņa[5], but I'm sure we will all be together again soon.[6] From what I could see, our departure really

---

[5] "Mamiņa" is the diminutive, affectionate form of "Mama".

[6] Nikolajs never did return to Latvia. As time passed, he seemed less and less
interested in going back, especially after his parents died.

37

pulled at Mamiņa's heart strings. Well, how could it not? Veltiņa and Wolfgang[7] also said their sad goodbyes. Wolfgang stated his intention to not go to Germany – they had to stay.

The sun is still shining on us warmly. The sun of our birthplace!

My precious bride has expressed a desire to partake in eating. No objections from me. We nosh on tomatoes, a boiled egg, etc..

All of a sudden, shots can be heard – we are experiencing the first air raid of our trip. So soon – still here in Riga. Let's hope it will be the last. Hurray! The ship is moving! Hah, it's not moving after all. We will have to keep waiting. It's already 17.00[8]. At least five hours have passed since all the travelers had to congregate. We don't even have access to our own

---

[7] Nikolajs' older sister, Velta and her husband, Wolfgang. "Veltiņa" is the diminutive, affectionate form of the name.
[8] Military time – 5:00pm. This format is used throughout the diary.

radio station. We can hear the news in German – no air raids are currently in progress over Germany.

Right now I may stop [writing], because nothing much is happening. I could eat a little, for what else can a person do on such a desolate ship. It's starting to get dark. We find a somewhat quiet corner away from the wind. We sit and talk about this and that. Also in our group is Mr. Velens and Mr. somebody else[9]. We drink something a little stronger and chat. Nearby another group is singing. The sound of beautiful Latvian songs fills the air.

It has become much darker and drowsiness is impudently creeping over me.

Somehow I will have to try and pretend to sleep. My wife and I lie down on something like a box lid, or a door. It's not especially comfortable, but we stay like this for a while. I must have fallen asleep, because suddenly I wake up. A cold

---

[9] Literally translated – apparently Nikolajs did not know this man's name.

wind is blowing and I am not feeling very good – something like a hangover. I forgot to mention that two alarms sounded during the night's darkness, although one was just a false alarm. Enemy Russians were throwing fire bombs somewhere near the shore not far from us and people are saying that some of them may have fallen dangerously close.

Since it is very cold, I, as the head of the family, have to concern myself with finding a warmer place to nestle. (The old lady has a toothache!)[10] I decide that a nearby lifeboat would be a fine place for us to climb into, because it would be much warmer inside and the wind would not get us! I pull my wife in after me and there we sleep until morning.

---

[10] This is one of many examples of Nikolajs' sarcastic humor in references to Erika. The term "old lady" is a loose translation of the Latvian word "vecenīte", a diminutive of the word "vecene", meaning old hag. It is being used in an idiomatic, almost endearing way and does not have a closer translation, since diminutives are not commonly used in English.

Escape from Latvia: My Father's Diary

September 8, 1944

I wake up. Nothing is amiss, feeling good, only my back is a bit flattened[11]. That's the floor's fault – it is very hard. The morning ablutions are followed by a robust breakfast – warm coffee, delicious bread with tomato, egg, roast chicken meat and finally, shortbread[12]. We see that our new discovery – the lifeboat – has turned out to be a very likeable location.

The wife is sleeping. I will have to join her. It is 8.10 and the wind is blowing hard against the deck. Good night!

---

[11] The actual word used was "nospiesta", a word with no direct translation appropriate to the specific usage. One has to imagine the effects on one's back of spending the night on the hard surface inside a lifeboat.

[12] The word used here, "biskvīts", might be taken to mean biscuit or cookie, but I have taken the liberty of translating it to "shortbread". My father often referred to this particular baked good during my childhood, although he never really claimed to have found an exact duplicate in Canada. According to Nikolajs, nothing was ever as good as it was back home.

Escape from Latvia: My Father's Diary

The time is 10.45. I stop rolling around on the floor, in other words, sleeping. I must admit our boat is very comfortable right now. Looking outside through the window[13], I can see it is very windy and the sea is quite rough. But I don't really even have to look – you can feel it rather well through the roof of our abode, i.e. the tarpaulin that is blowing and fluttering in the wind. Passengers are standing around on the deck, frozen in the wind, noses red. It turns out the convoy[14] isn't traveling in one row, but in two, that is, one next to the other. Supposedly, that is safer. One can see one or two weaker individuals who are suffering with so-called sea sickness. It's not pleasant to suffer, of course – my sympathies! But my other half only sleeps and reads "Lagerlefi"[15]. What a lovable and calm little

---

[13] Not sure if the lifeboat really had a window, or if he was simply looking out over the edge and this is a metaphor for the lifeboat serving as a house with a window.

[14] This is the only reference to the ship being part of a convoy and no other information is available.

[15] No reference available – perhaps this was a newspaper or magazine.

bug[16]. A circumstance worthy of note happens about 12:00 noon: my wife joins the legions of the seasick. She struggles miserably on all fours in our luxury yacht. How sorry I feel for her. But my powers are very weak – I have no way of helping her. Maybe eating would help. I give her a sour pickle, some meat. Apparently this helps. And now she is sleeping again. Let her sleep[17]. Outside the sun is shining, but the sea is still banging around. I will have to start reading my book[18].

Erika is still having problems in the afternoon. Death is likely.[19] After all, the waves are rocking the ship slightly. I go out on the deck and look around at the more noteworthy areas, that is, those spots containing more of the sufferers – the bow

---

[16] "Bug" is a literal translation for what is clearly an endearment.

[17] At this point in time, Erika would have been 2 to 2-1/2 months pregnant, but we have no indication that her symptoms were anything but seasickness. It's possible she would have felt the same on dry land.

[18] Nikolajs never mentions the name of the book, but it may have been Theodore Dreiser's "An American Tragedy", since that's what Erika was reading later in the diary. It's not likely they had many books with them.

[19] Another example of Nikolajs' sarcasm.

and stern of the ship. The sights are interesting- too bad they can't be captured for posterity[20].

It is evening. Will have to go to sleep – the wife is not the only sleepy one. Sweet dreams!

September 9, 1944.

I wake up around 6. It is still sort of dark, but I am curious to see how far we have sailed. I hear we are in Gotenhafen[21]. Will have to believe it. People on the deck are becoming more animated, louder.

It has become even lighter. I can see the ship's fires. It is possible to make out silhouettes of submarines and ships that are becoming more visible by the moment. Now it is much brighter and we are sailing into the port of Danzig. The sights are unseen and, therefore, interesting. On the shore can be

---

[20] Nikolajs would have liked to sketch some of the people as he was often known to do in the presence of interesting faces.
[21] At the time, located in German controlled Prussia, now Gdynia in Poland.

seen huge cranes, all the harbor equipment, various shipping company buildings and, farther down, factory smokestacks. Our large watercraft is assisted by tugboats.

Finally, we climb down off the ship Moero[22]. This is followed by the craziest ever baggage unloading and pickup. The sequence is like this: bags are unloaded and then each person can take what he or she wants unless the rightful owner grabs one by the collar. We hang around the harbor all day until finally we obtain our miniscule possessions.

Then we are once again on the train and the first destination is said to be Stargard[23]. The train ride seemed endless, especially since the conditions were not at all conducive to sleeping.

---

[22] http://www.wrecksite.eu/wreck.aspx?15307 The Moero was sunk by Soviet planes in an air raid near Riga, Latvia on September 22, 1944, 13 days after Nikolajs and Erika debarked in Danzig.
[23] A city in the Polish province of Pomerania.

September 10, 1944

We ride and ride. My wife tells me that, in the darkness, she saw beautiful scenery all around. How could she see that in the dark?[24]

It is getting much lighter. In our car, at the other end, some motivated German cronies have been singing non-stop for over an hour.

The wife isn't leaving me alone, she has to eat. I guess I am under her thumb[25] - I obey. The trip continues along the seacoast and our next destination is Berlin.

The surrounding countryside is bleak and doesn't present any surprises. Broad fields, scorched in the dry weather, alternate with young forests[26].

---

[24] Erika may have seen, or imagined, but she might have simply been demonstrating her youthful enthusiasm.
[25] Literal translation of the phrase he used: "under her slipper"
[26] Germany has acres of neatly planted trees in various stages of growth that are replacements for areas of deforestation due to various causes, including farming, destruction in wartime, etc.

First of all we are delayed in Stargard. Pretty little town. Near the station are gardens abundant with apples and pears. This phenomenon has been evident anywhere we have been in Germany[27]. It is already dark as we approach Berlin. Another air raid! The train stops somewhere in the woods. In the distance we can see *artillery firing at enemy bombers*[28]. After a little while we are able to continue the trip.

Berlin 1944[29]

---

[27] Stargard was located in Poland in 1944, but borders were shifting due to German occupation, so it may have, indeed, been Germany at that time.
[28] Liberties taken with translation.
[29] berlin kantstraße 1944 www.produktive-medienarbeit.de No doubt a typical view of German cities in 1944.

We are in Berlin. It is dark, but we can see silhouettes of bombed buildings. Then starts the crazy walking and riding the U-bahn[30] in all directions.

September 11, 1944

It's 6.30. We are sitting on the train that is bringing us to Wuppertal. The surroundings are simply nasty! They can't be compared with Latvia at all. On the way we ride past different stations and our first stop – only Hanover. It should be noted that, from what we saw of Berlin's buildings as we rode by, they were, without exception, more or less destroyed in air raids.

---

[30] Subway

Hanover 1939[31]

Then about Hanover, Hanover is a very beautiful city, with beautiful paved streets and beautiful modern structures. Unfortunately, it, too, has suffered from air raids and many buildings have crumbled

---

[31] www.heimatsammlung.de Hanover 1939

Hanover 1944[32]

Starting with Hanover, the surroundings are becoming more attractive, as are the houses. We also aren't seeing as many multi-family houses, which we don't like. Many beautiful trees, such as poplar, silver willows, etc..

Another air raid. The train stops and we wait for the end of the alarm. But more bad luck – between us and our destination, the railroad tracks have been damaged, perhaps in

---

[32] bergen-belsen.stiftung-ng.de Hanover 1944

an air raid. We have to go out of our way to get around the problem. We are so tired of this train ride and our moods are almost at zero.

Farmers, evidently knowing we would ride by and wanting to tempt us terribly, have hung many, many apples in the trees by the side of the tracks[33]. It turns out that, in Germany, apple trees are planted alongside roads and the ones we are seeing were so planted.

After the longest stretch, we are in Wuppertal. This city, too, is in ruins. We are greeted by.....no one. We stand there with our baggage and wonder. Somebody comes up with the idea to call the factory[34], so someone can come and meet us. A guard type arrives on a bicycle. The factory is a fifteen-minute walk – at most. We start to go. Once fifteen minutes

---

[33] This sentence should be read as sarcasm.

[34] It becomes clear later in the diary that the refugees are being sponsored by the factory in which they will be working, probably Espenlaube (see notes p. 18).

have [*Erika picks up mid-sentence at this point*[35]] *long passed, even then we are far from the end. It turns out that our future workplace and domicile are still farther ahead. Along the way we ponder and think, everything seems worse than it really is.*

As soon as we arrive in the factory, we are offered beer, we are able to wash up, and afterwards we are also able to get dinner. After all these sleepless nights, we are very tired and soon we go to rest. We have to spend this night in barracks, where Russians are living next door[36]. Our accommodations consist of two-story bunk beds, but soon we have almost forgotten all the difficulties of the trip and we sleep in peace.

---

[35] Erika's script will be different to distinguish when she makes entries. No mention is made as to why she has started writing. They alternate until September 29, Erika's last entry. From October 7 to the end, only Nikolajs contributes.

[36] A somewhat surprising fact that German DP camps contain Russians, but self-explanatory when one knows about the devastation caused by Stalin.

Escape from Latvia: My Father's Diary

September 12, 1944

*(Erika) We awoke fairly early.[37] Outside the air seems rather
cool, therefore, too, we are not feeling especially joyous. While we are eating
breakfast in the dining hall, we run into Egonis[38], a truly happy event.
We follow Egonis to the camp where we find Elvira. We are very surprised
at the barracks, at least, I don't know what Koļa[39] (Nikolajs) is thinking,
because he hasn't told me what that is[40]. Koļa and Egonis go to the factory
and we walk towards town. One can get delicious ice cream there, but this
time we were unlucky, because we were surprised by an alarm in the city
and the only thing we could do was turn around and go back.*

---

[37] The constant changing of tense from past to present and back is a direct
translation of Erika's writing. I have taken the liberty of adding punctuation to
improve readability, because she seemed to have her own way of creating
long, run-on sentences without commas or periods.

[38] Egonis is the husband of Elvira, Erika's best friend from high school. His
name is listed both as "Egonis" and "Egons"; both are seemingly correct.

[39] Nikolajs' nickname in Latvian.

[40] This apparent lack of communication lasted throughout their marriage. In
this case, Nikolajs might have said nothing so as not to upset Erika, which she
misinterpreted as not talking to her. Each one expected the other to read his
or her mind.

Escape from Latvia: My Father's Diary

Koļa and Egonis return in the afternoon and we tour Wuppertal's better sights, especially the ice cream store, and afterwards, we eat dinner. It's very pleasant[41] here – for example, at least everything is very clean and service is very polite. Beer is most plentiful. It's not "Pelonis"[42], but unfortunately we will probably soon tire of it.

September 13, 1944

(Erika) Today is another restless morning. All around us, our neighbors are getting up early and Koļa also gets up. He and Egons head to the station to unload train cars. Today I have enough work at home, because our surroundings aren't very pleasant[43] so at least I will straighten up. Later I am going to go and type a little, because Mr. Velens has his

---

[41] Loosely translated. The word in Latvian, "omulīgs" does not have an accurate counterpart in English, but is usually used to describe a warm, cozy atmosphere.

[42] Must have been a popular Latvian beer.

[43] Again, the term "omulīgs" was used, in this case more likely representing niceness more than warmth or coziness and, again, without a direct translation.

54

hands full with work right now[44]. So I do this and that and the day goes by unnoticed. In the evening we go and eat fried potatoes and sausages, which taste pretty good. Afterwards, Egons, Elvira and Koļa play cards and so ends this day's celebration.

September 14, 1944

(Nikolajs) This morning it is raining. What unpleasant weather. Erika is so cranky and she seems to be doing her best to ruin my mood. Good luck! She tells me I eat too much. This is not true, I eat as little as a baby chick. And then these constant reprimands. Today I noticed the first few grey hairs at my temples. Those I will carefully cover with dye.

Right now things are more or less peaceful, a result of having eaten some bread and jam.

---

[44] Erika often refers to people and events without providing a context, so the fact that she is typing for one of the men on the boat may appear to be random.

September 15, 1944

(Nikolajs) Once again, I am offered a job working on building barracks. How could I decline? My assignment is to climb on the roof and, where the boards have not yet been nailed down, to do so. Three of us are on the roof, two Latvians and one Italian. I try to converse with the Italian and it's not even so disastrous – he understands a little if I speak German. He is from Bologna and has been in the war for five years. The war will be over in a month – so he thinks.[45] Let it be so, as he says. At 5 o'clock we finish work.

September 16, 1944

(Erika) This morning everybody has arisen early. Koļa and the other men go to work – apparently to build barracks. A guard has come for all the wives who, up till now, were lazing around, and tells us to hurry. Everyone to the factory and without delay, register for work. So, I rush to

---

[45] It would take another 9 months before the war in Europe would end, but the Italian's prescience is notable.

the factory. We have to go to the personnel department head. All the women are assigned to work. I am the only one who escapes free, hurray!!![46]

September 17, 1944

(Erika) Today is Sunday. At least we can sleep in properly. Today we have plans to go to the Wuppertal Zoo. We ride a streetcar; the trip is rather long. Finally we are at the end. The surroundings are lovely: wide streets, beautiful houses, and farther on we can see tree covered hills. First we see the zoo restaurant. It's a huge building with beautiful gardens full of fields of especially colorful flowers. The overall sight is wonderful. Up till now, nothing we have seen has left us with a particularly gracious impression, but today's sights truly make us acknowledge the often heard observations about Wuppertal's beautiful environs.

---

[46] Erika appears to be happy not to have to work.

Wuppertal zoo 1881[47]

Lunch was also not bad. After stuffing ourselves[48], we went to look at the few remaining animals[49]. The most beautiful of what was left was the aquarium and, besides that, a few monkeys, crocodiles, etc.. After a long walk in the zoo, we went into the café to drink a cup and have some torte.

---

[47] www.zoo-wuppertal.de
[48] Literally translated, "terrible eating".
[49] Wuppertal Zoo was partially destroyed in the war, but reopened a few days after it ended.

After living it up we drove[50] to the city and indulged in freshly made ice cream. Afterwards, right next door at a movie theatre, we saw some sort of criminal film.

September 18, 1944

(Erika) The day is once again like all the others. Nothing special; I go grocery shopping; today Koļa is working. Somehow the day goes by quickly, I probably have to get used to housekeeping.

September 19, 1944

(Erika) This morning we received our baggage from Danzig harbor. Seems like a few things "fell out".[51] Too bad! – yes, Koļa is angry again, that's how it is every day.

---

[50] This is the first indication that they are in a car, although no mention is made as to who is driving. The Latvian word, "brauc" is the same for "rode" and "drove", so it may have been a streetcar.

[51] This may have been where they "lost" their wedding rings.

Escape from Latvia: My Father's Diary

September 20, 1944

(Erika) I must be getting used to this lazy life. In the morning I sleep until 8, that is so beautiful. Sometimes I even get angry with those who are making noise around us so early in the morning. Everything else is the same as usual, I go grocery shopping, later to lunch, supper we eat at home. Today I heard people talking that the Russians are 8 kilometers from Riga. Here we are living as if we were in a sack. We don't read newspapers, because we haven't seen any for sale. We have not been able to locate Riga radio, so we have to survive on rumors.

September 21, 1944

(Erika) Today is very foggy — through the window you can see only mountains of fog and it even feels as if the fog is pushing its way into the room through the open window. Will have to go to lunch. Koļa is working so very hard.

Friday, September 22, 1944

(Nikolajs) Today something happened that I was trying hard all along to avoid – I have been assigned to the "2 verka"[52]. Yes, what can I do, now I will have to work 72 hours a week.

September 23, 1944

(Nikolajs) I stand in front of the chief and the rest of the workers of the 2 verka – Arbeitsvorbereitung[53] - led by Miller. I am assigned to inspection of wing steering mechanisms. I am introduced to several German girls – company workers. Lively girls, those Germans. One is named Gerda, and she shows me photographs of the Tyrol region.

---

[52] The closest I have been able to interpret this is that he was assigned to a particular division of the factory.
[53] Translates as "preparation for work" or "planning"

Tyrol region 1944[54]

At approximately 21.30 the radio reports that enemy planes are attacking Darmstadt and Dusseldorf. In the distance we hear the roar of aircraft and the firing of artillery[55]. Dusseldorf is approximately 30 km. from Wuppertal, so that's why we can hear everything so well. The air attack comes in several waves and the bombing lasts about an hour. We can see flames from where bombs have hit. We only go to bed around 24.00.

---

[54] www.bevaringsprogram.lund.se
[55] The specific word used was "zenitartilerija", literally "zenith artillery".

Sunday, September 24, 1944

(Nikolajs) Cool morning. Many have arisen very early and are running down the hall in wooden shoes. I should take a rifle and shoot them. *(Erika) The noise really is terrible, even I must get up. We eat lunch at "Krota"[56], because it has decided to rain. After lunch, Kola and Egons drive to the "zoo" for cakes, and we brew coffee. So we spend Sunday in peace.*

September 25, 1944

(Erika) For me all the days are the same. In the mornings I go for milk and to shop in the other stores. The rest of the time I read T. Dreiser's, "An American Tragedy".

September 26, 1944

(Erika) As I said, my days are all evenly grey. I am tormented by my foul mood and this is amplified by my mean nature, that always makes Kola angry with me. It's really terrible, but it's probably both our

---

[56] No indication what or where "Krota" is, but it may be a dining hall.

faults. It's sad that, after 6 long months of togetherness we can't stand each other and to control ourselves we have to clench our teeth. It happens, too, that after all the day's chores, spent together with nice ladies, the evenings seem unbearable, in the company of a wife such as me. I don't know if in all this I am entirely to blame. It can be said that one can feel sincerely sorry for those people who make a mistake![57]

September 27, 1944

(Erika) The question of my working still has not been resolved. It's possible that I may have to work, even all day.[58] *I am not unhappy about that, at least not right now, because I am tired of being alone all day and not seeing anyone, at least if the surroundings were more pleasant. Outside for the most part is very cool, so that, too, is out. Koļa is gone all day, with time I will probably even forget what he looks like, not to talk about him already; among other things, even today I love Koļa very much*

---

[57] Erika seems to be feeling sorry for herself, but she does realize that perhaps Nikolajs overreacts.
[58] Initially Erika was happy not to have to work.

and, if, sometimes, I dwell on memories, then I have to admit that, in spite of all the calamities, I am happy.

September 28, 1944

(Erika) This morning I was very sleepy, but I can't sleep any longer, because Dr. Bardins promised to come this morning. Having come in, he related that Dr. Lange said I have to work after all, but they can't force me, if I absolutely don't want to. Tomorrow I will go and have my lungs checked, we will see what will happen after that.

September 29, 1944[59]

Saturday, October 7, 1944

(Nikolajs) I haven't written for a long time, because it simply was not possible. Work ends at 20.00, I eat supper until 20.30, then a couple of days I have to shave. Now when would I have time to write?

---

[59] Erika's last entry.

Every day and night we have alarms and have to hurry to the air raid shelter in a bunker. Neighboring cities such as Bochum, Dusseldorf, Krefeld, Duisburg, Krefeld (*sic*) and others are experiencing significant bombings every day. But luck is smiling on our Wuppertal. We will see how long. Thursday evening another 147 Latvians arrive, from whom only 20 are workers from the old Espenlaube.

A few days ago Erika and Elvira rode[60] to a small town – Leichlingen – where they bought green pears. After they are allowed to ripen for a few days, they taste quite splendid. And now I am going to write a little about the ration cards we were issued.

First of all, each of us is given – Wachenkarte für ausländische Zivilarbeiter – for one week. On each card, one

---

[60] Method of transportation unspecified.

can receive 650 grams of white bread, 1800 grams of something resembling our "breijatai"[61] bread.

An example of a ration card[62]

About the white bread it can be said, it is truly marvelous, almost like that at home in peace time.

Then 225 grams of sugar, so in a month that amounts to 900 grams, that is, twice as much as in Latvia. Then 2.5 kilograms of potatoes, 250 grams of meat, 175 grams of marmalade, 35 grams of margarine, 62.5 grams of cottage cheese (already prepared – thick milk), 62.5 grams of coffee, 150 grams

---

[61] A specific kind of bread – no translation available.
[62] https://www.huesken.com/shop/en/german-nazi-history-1933-1945-ten/lebensmittel-wochenkarte-48235.html

– Nährmittel – macaroni, rice or cream of wheat. With butter, up till now it was like this, that we could get 125 grams, but right now butter is being completely substituted with margarine.

Then men can also receive 80 cigarettes per month on smoking cards. Women can receive cigarettes if they are older than 25. My wife is not!

Each person is also given a slip with which one can register with a shoemaker for repairs.

Oh, I forgot the milk cards. Each of us receives ¼ liter of milk per day that has such a blue tint, it's a joy to look at. In other words, especially skimmed skim milk.

Sunday, October 8, 1944

(Nikolajs) We sleep late, because last night we went to bed late. The clock reads 9.30 when we start to get up. I completely forgot to say that we have moved to another apartment – we are living together with Mr. Vizbulis' family. We sleep on

two stories, the wives upstairs, we, the heads of household, on the lower level. We sleep in beds into which have been placed some straw, so they make a somewhat hard place to sleep.

Today we took an excursion on the Bergbahn[63] into the mountains; even there everything is destroyed.

Bergbahn 1944[64]

---

[63] A railway climbing up to the top of a mountain. Several can be found in Germany, but Nikolajs does not specify which one they rode, so the photograph is only an example.

[64] http://www.bing.com/im-ages/search?q=bergbahn+1944&qpvt=bergbahn+1944&qpvt=bergbahn+1944&qpvt=bergbahn+1944&FORM=IQFRML

We can see that this used to be a neighborhood of summer homes, because from the ruins one can imagine the reconstruction of beautiful houses. Near some of the homes can be seen garages containing burned out cars. In the mountain restaurant[65] we eat cakes and drink bean coffee[66].

Postcard of mountain restaurant

---

[65] The postcard photo is of the restaurant on a mountain near Wuppertal, perhaps the very same one in which they sat. http://www.bing.com/images/search?q=1944%20wuppertal%20bergbahn&qs=n&form=QBIRMH&sp=-1&pq=1944%20wuppertal%20bergbahn&sc=0-23&sk=&cvid=BF46D2E6E3FA4459993FAF70D2E6D3EF

[66] "Real" coffee made of coffee beans was scarce.

Escape from Latvia: My Father's Diary

Monday, October 9, 1944

(Nikolajs) At night on my way home from work sirens are blowing a full alarm. The radio announces that bigger formations are attacking Wuppertal. Everybody hurries to the bunker and we, too, join the terrified crowd. The enemy hangs all kinds of colorful little fires from the clouds. The air hums from the airplane engines. I have to think there are many of them. Thank God, all ended well; only the electric power station was bombed and all of Wuppertal was shrouded in darkness.

Tuesday, October 10, 1944

(Nikolajs) I always think and think about home. What are my dear Mamiņa, papucīts[67], Veltiņa, little Andris doing? I look at my mother's photograph and tears fill my eyes. I can't

---

[67] Diminutive of "papus", or father.

get the picture out of my mind of my mother standing on the shore as we were leaving.

How are things going in Riga? Right now the last group of people from Latvia has arrived – Estonians and Germans who worked in Spilve[68]. All citizens of Riga have to evacuate.

Monday, October 10, 1944

(Nikolajs) Finally, we receive the long-awaited letter from home (dated 19 September). Mamiņa was probably rushing to send a letter since she really didn't end up writing much. Mamiņa writes that Veltiņa left Latvia on September 21, going where she does not know; probably to Salzburg. But the most important thing she writes is that my father, mother and Andris

---

[68] Spilve Airport is a former civilian and military airport in Latvia located 5 km north of Riga city centre, from which aircraft took off as early as the First World War. Wikipedia.

72

have to leave the house on September 30, in other words, evacuate. I don't know where my dear parents are going to be sent now. But no doubt God will stand by them.

Tonight Erika has cooked a magnificent supper – potatoes, herring pudding and pear "kīselis"[69] with cream of wheat. I ate too much. We washed it all down with tasty beer.

Another thing, the technical director of GMBH[70], Zimmerman, personally invited me into the construction office and informed me that, very soon, we would be moving somewhere south. In other words, farther away from Espenlaube!

Sunday, November 12, 1944

(Nikolajs) Haven't written for quite a stretch – should give it a try. Today we sleep in until 10.00 and feel like it is

---

[69] A common Latvian dessert, fruit soup/compote thickened with potato flour or corn starch.

[70] For one description of what this means, go to: http://www.investopedia.com/ask/answers/05/051305.asp

Sunday. My little wife has caught a terrible chill with a cold and a bad cough. And this is all because we haven't received our box[71] and the wife[72] doesn't have anything to wear. When will we finally receive our belongings? Outside it is so cold and it is raining again. It is like that every day. Wuppertal is in third place in the world for annual rainfall. But maybe we will be able to get away from this unfortunate place. Director Mann stated that, at the latest 4 weeks from now, we, that is, Potempo[73] people will be heading somewhere southward. The place is currently secret, but some people have speculated that we will go somewhere southeast, not far from Bairotra[74] and 120 versts[75]

---

[71] Not sure where the box was coming from, but it seems as if it were to contain warm clothing.

[72] The term used was "vecenite", described earlier as the untranslatable diminutive of old lady.

[73] Difficult to ascertain meaning, but may be a reference to the Polish word, "potempa", meaning condemned.

[74] Unable to find anything close – perhaps he meant Bayreuth, but that is in northern Bavaria and not the southeast near Switzerland.

[75] Verst definition, a Russian measure of distance equivalent to 3500 feet or 0.6629 mile or 1.067 kilometers.

from Swiss borders. Supposedly it is a nice place. Let's hope. For three weeks I have been working at the third verka. I really don't like it there. All of the verka is one high shack surrounded by field guns. But what can I do, I have to work. During this time bombs fell on Wuppertal and the surrounding area. And last night was the biggest bombing of all near us. The worst part is that they let us out of verka only for severe alarms. Yesterday, as soon as the severe alarm sounded, bombs were dropping not far from us. We fly as fast as possible to the bunker.

German field gun[76]

---

[76] militaryhistoryofthe20thcentury.blogspot.com

In the end, the outcome was approximately like this: one bunker was destroyed (later some bodies were discovered), in the neighborhood one house burned down, several were hit, many windows were broken. Then bombs were also dropped on the railroad line, which was probably the main target of the bombing.

At night we once again make our way to the bunker, because the air above Wuppertal is full of Tommies[77]. Solingen really suffered and that's why today the verka didn't provide lunch – that was sent to the victims of Solingen's air raid.

We haven't received any response from Velta, don't know what has happened to her. But let's hope it turns out to be the fault of the post office.

---

[77] Nikolajs' name for British forces – a reference to Tommy guns.

Sunday, December 10, 1944

(Nikolajs) Time is flying on the wings of the wind, but new events refuse to transpire. We are still in the same unpleasant Wuppertal where it rains all the time, freezing and having to traipse through wet, muddy roads. Tonight about 5 centimeters of snow fell, but unfortunately, it can't even be called snow, more like a white colored watery gruel.

We still have not received our box and the hopes of receiving it are growing ever dimmer. It is a very miserable thing that depresses and about which one must always wonder. Erika suffers from this the most, because she doesn't have anything to wear, and has to walk around in a thin summer coat. What follows are a cold, bad cough, toothache and other things. When will it all be different, when will we receive it? Christmas is right around the corner, but what will it bring us this year? What will it be like this year here in Wuppertal?

After the holidays a group of about 30 people will be going in advance of everyone else to the new workplace in

Bairotra. We will probably not be among these lucky ones, because this group will consist of couples both of whom are working, unmarried men and couples without children. If only we could get away from this hell once and for all!

We received a letter from Wolfgang in which he writes that Veltiņa is in Salzburg, but, unfortunately, she has to be in a hospital bed. During an air raid, finding herself in a shelter, she became very sick and was taken to a hospital. Wolfgang writes that Veltiņas health is very bad and one lung is completely non-functional. How could she, poor girl, be doing well, by herself in a strange part of the world, away from her mother's care, that would be so necessary now. She must be thinking of her Andrejs[78], her parents, her homeland, worrying, and that is all having a bad effect on her health.

---

[78] Earlier in the diary, Nikolajs refers to his nephew as "Andris", but this time he changed it to Andrejs, which, I believe, is correct.

We are also quite far away from her and can't help her at all. Then again, we couldn't do much, but at least she might be less lonely.

And what is little Andrejs doing, and Mamiņa and papucis. I have the feeling that they are still at home on Dzutes Street and maybe they are doing better than we are. But it is hard for Mamiņa when we are away; she always has to think about us and how things are going for us in a strange place. Will we ever see each other again and, if so, when will that be? But I am an optimist and I can't even imagine that we will never see each other again.

The days drag at work, but the weeks fly quickly. If only some sort of compromise would happen in the overall political situation and clear up our status; of course it would have to be in our favor.

Sunday, December 24, 1944

(Nikolajs) Hurray! At last we received our long-awaited box. That happy circumstance happened Tuesday, December 19, in the darkness of evening, when they brought over the crate from the first verka on a hand truck. The box, it turns out, was not pilfered during its journey, but that part of the crate containing foodstuffs could be deemed to be in total chaos. The cream of wheat had to be thrown out completely, the container of barley had suffered immensely, the bag of sugar had leaked out and from 3 kilograms of sugar, only one was left. The barley had suffered immensely, also we had to throw away a lot of the peas. And the fault of all this lay with the tomatoes and cucumbers.

Now a little bit about the worst disaster. Turns out that we put our "okstiņus"[79] in the produce compartment and they

---

[79] Unable to find a translation, but the context appears to have it refer to personal items of some sort.

were simply in a catastrophic state. But what to do, it's my own fault. All the rest of our clothes and undergarments were in perfect condition. So all in all everything is in pretty good order and we are satisfied.

Tonight is Christmas Eve[80] and Erika and I were in church. Germans, it turns out, are good singers and sing songs to a faster tempo than in Latvian churches. On the altar sparkles a shining Christmas tree.[81]

We come home from church to some gifts.[82] My wife presented me with a splendid ashtray, although I have become less of a smoker. Elvira gave me a pencil[83] and Lisija[84] a wall calendar. Erika received a powder box from Elvira and, from

---

[80] Many European Christians celebrate Christmas on December 24.

[81] Christmas being such an emotional time for me, I can't imagine the feelings going through Nikolajs and Erika as they sat gazing at the brightly lit tree on the altar so far away from home.

[82] Traditional sequence of events on Christmas Eve – church, gift opening, dinner (sometimes eaten before church).

[83] Nikolajs was an artist, so this was clearly a very meaningful gift.

[84] First mention of this unidentified woman.

Lisija, a Carl Raddatz[85] genealogy enlargement. I gave Erika two brooches. An "eglite"[86] for Latvians was organized in the adjacent barracks. The Lagerfuhrer[87], Tivisen, spoke, followed by Rev. Lappuķe. We sang Christmas songs[88].

This was followed by a Christmas feast, of course, each of us in our own room with our family; now Erika would over-feed me. There was roast pork meat, fried sausages, sauerkraut, potatoes; then Berlin pancakes[89] with buttermilk[90]. I was stuffed to the gills.[91]

---

[85] A German stage and film actor.

[86] Traditional Latvian Christmas party, often held at the church and something I attended every year until I left home. Food, singing, and Santa handing out gifts to the children, who had to perform a song or poem to earn the gift.

[87] Camp Leader.

[88] The Latvian word, "dziesmas", can be used for "songs", "carols", and "hymns", so it is unclear which were being sung at the party.

[89] A traditional German dessert.

[90] The actual words used here translate to "fermented milk".

[91] Idiomatic translation of "overate to my throat".

I went in to Williamson's – that poor boy was thrown by himself into the turmoil[92] - forever hurt. We agreed on a three-handed game. A three-handed game became a five-handed game, since Elvira, Lisija and Egons didn't go visiting. On Christmas Day we slept late, ate well and a lot, played some cards. The day after[93] was spent in much the same way. The menu was approximately like this:

1. Christmas Day dinner: Rolmopsi[94] with potatoes and debesu manna[95] with milk.

2. Second Christmas dinner: konzervi[96] with potatoes and bread soup[97].

---

[92] Literal translation of "lasa čaka" is something like "salmon eddy".

[93] Or "second Christmas", celebrated in some countries as Boxing Day.

[94] Slices of beef are pounded, filled with whatever is available (breadcrumbs, carrots, pickles, bacon), rolled, then secured with string; stewed in broth until tender; gravy is thickened and seasoned.

[95] A dessert made with fruit juice thickened with cream of wheat, then whipped until light and fluffy.

[96] Some kind of unspecified preserved meat.

[97] May have been a milk-based, sweetened cold dessert soup, but no details are available.

Let's not talk about supper, that in itself was understandably on one's own.

December 31, 1944 – New Year's Eve

(Nikolajs) On New Year's Eve we were first of all greeted by rather powerful bombing. We got to go to the bunker. We welcomed in the New Year at home, quietly and peacefully. On the morning of January 1, all the younger men were called outside near the barracks, where they were hailed as recruits into air defense military service. The assignment – to attend to zenith big guns for the second and third verka. I was put in there, too. At night, once again the Tommies[98] threatened us terribly and it turns out that in Vohwinkel[99] about 2,000 70 kilogram bombs were dropped.

---

[98] The British.
[99] A subdivision of Wuppertal.

Escape from Latvia: My Father's Diary

February 4, 1945

(Nikolajs) Well, what a crazy thing – I look on our one conspicuous piece of furniture (a cupboard combined with a nightstand) and see that a layer of dust about one centimeter thick has collected on my diary. Who is to blame – me, or perhaps the Mrs. – the dustcloth disappeared three weeks ago. I turn the pages and it turns out that the last time I wrote was on New Year's Day. Nothing much has happened in our family since then. The most notable happening is that we received two letters from Veltiņa. The first was written on December 2 – last year and the second on January 23. Things have been all over the place for my sister and of course, not as well as was planned out in Latvia. Nothing materialized at Madame Risa's in Salzburg and Velta got a job in some outfit preparing bandages[100]. After a few days, Salzburg was hit by heavy enemy air raids. Velta got to hurry to a bunker inside a mountain cave. At

---

[100] Literal translation: sanitary wrappings.

one point the oxygen apparatus failed – people were unable to breathe, and my poor sister lost consciousness and had to be brought to the hospital. She was bleeding heavily and the doctor determined that both lungs were damaged – an old ailment.

Convinced by Wolfgang, Velta is taken to Dresden to Wolfgang's parents and there she is still. She is taking sleeping cures, eating and doing well. If only it were that way.

Both of us are still in the same unhappy Wuppertal. Still nothing has happened with Bayreuth and probably never will. Erikiņa[101] is not doing well, she has heartburn and all kinds of similar misfortunes. But surely one day things will be better. Will have to stop writing, getting sleepy, because the time is just about 22.00.

---

[101] The diminutive, affectionate form of Erika, an early indication that Nikolajs has softened with respect to his wife.

Thursday, February 22, 1945

(Nikolajs) All kinds of new events have taken place during this short time. Once again we received two letters from Veltina. One was not a letter, but notification that we have to go to the post office to pick up a money order – 150 Reichmarks. Oh you dear little[102] sister! After that we received a letter in which Veltiņa, from her poverty, sent us 5 kilograms of bread – in coupons. How well she thinks of us and how is she getting by, since she only has ration cards, too? So when we are together again in our homeland I will do my best to pay her back.

Another big event – the first group left last week for Bairotra (Goldmüll)[103]. There is hope that perhaps, too, we will eventually end up there.

---

[102] Not to mean "younger", since Velta was the older sibling.
[103] This location has not been verified, but Goldmull may have been the name of a factory

The warring all around us has become particularly intense. The firing of big guns is heard throughout the night and the air raids are coming closer and closer to us. Every day they hit Dusseldorf, Duisburg, Essen, Bochum, Cologne, Krefeld. "Jagdbombers"[104] float up everywhere, often in Wuppertal. Right near here in Schwelm, last week Latvian barracks were hit and one family named Umbraško was completely destroyed – father, son and mother. The only one left alive was a little girl. The rest of the Latvians suffered heavy losses – some were left with only the clothes on their backs.

Eating, too, is becoming sadder – now the 4 week ration cards have to last 5 weeks. Crazy.[105]

---

[104] A fighter-bomber is a fighter aircraft that is modified or used primarily as a light bomber in the tactical bombing and ground attack roles. Wikipedia.com

[105] I remember my father relating the story of him and others sneaking into farmers' fields at night to steal potatoes, because they had so little to eat.

Thursday, April 5, 1945

(Nikolajs) First of all, we have survived two attacks – the first was on March 13 and the second on March 19. The first air raid on the 13th cut a wide swath and hit all of Wuppertal. I was in a rock bunker where it was almost completely safe, although with an unpleasant feeling. Things were much worse for Erika – at the time she was somewhere near the Langerfeld market and getting to the Luftschutz bunker was out of the question. She had ducked into a basement and, luckily, my little old lady escaped unharmed. When all the bombing stopped, the realization came that bombs had fallen everywhere, even high in the mountains that contain only private homes. Many dead, the first verka was hit, the third also partly in ruins, only the second left undamaged. Bombs had definitely fallen all around. Especially many on the air field next to the second verka. Wuppertal was completely in flames. The worst part was that the barracks directly next to ours were hit and one bomb was particularly close. Our room was no longer a room – it was

a pile of boards, the roof caved in, straw in everything and a mix of clay and sand. Some of the Latvians were living next to the second verka in what was once a school building. Now we were forced to move in there, too. We gathered together the most precious of what was left of our riches. It must be said that God was standing with us and that is because Mamiņa is praying for us.

The second air raid, in other words, bombing, came on very suddenly and I had just managed to run down into the school's basement, because they say it is safer, after all, in basements than attics during bombing. At the time, Erikiņa was a couple of hundred meters from the school building in a store and also ended up in the basement. It was crazy. The following were bombarded: the second verka, the railroad, and here and there. The air raid[106] happened in several waves and later it

---

[106] Allied bombing was escalating; this was just weeks before the Americans came in.

turned out that about 30 bombs fell one after another right near the school building. The school building itself was not damaged – an annex containing a gym was hit by a folltrefer[107]. Dust and chalk fell and I thought for sure that the final hour was near. When all the fun was over, all that was left to do was to thank God that he saved us and to wonder how we managed to stay alive.

We also received signs of life from Veltiņa, written from Possendorf near Dresden. The content was like this: Dresden has burned down, including our house. Lives were saved. Write!

Yes, I don't know what's going on with my dear sister right now. I'm convinced, after all, that everything will be all right and we will all see each other in our beloved homeland.

---

[107] The only place this term was found on the Internet was a site in Polish related to 1944 wartime activity, so it may have been a specific type of missile or bomb.

The biggest event after all took place on March 25, exactly on Palm Sunday morning, when the stork brought my wife little Ilze. That was only a happy occasion – hurray I am a father! The fact took place in Schwelm's hospital – Marienen hospital.[108] My wife had a hard time during labor and was pale and weak. I found a baby carriage to buy and so, on second Easter[109] the three of us returned from Schwelm to Wuppertal. Then the difficult days began, because food was scarce and, besides that, there was no peace from the enemy. Always, the camp announcement and running to the bunker.[110] Then events started to develop at a much faster pace. Artillery started to fire, then Flatingen was occupied, then Schwelm, and on

---

[108] Very little information is available about this facility, but a hospital currently exists in Schwelm, HELIOS, that may have grown out of the one that was there in 1945.

[109] Presumably the Monday after Easter.

[110] The original sentence contains words for which no translation was found, so liberties were taken with context: *"Vienmer kampverbaudas un jaboš un uz bunkuru nenoskrieties."*

April 15 the Americans marched into Wuppertal.[111] All of it materialized very simply and without shadows. There was only some minor artillery fire. We got to smoke some Camels and other fine American cigarettes. The next morning, Russians living in the area started looting the stores and quickly emptied the shops on Langerfeld Street. After all that, we were left with crumbs and now, thanks to God, we are eating much better.

---

[111] Clearly this was written after April 15, but the date of writing was not changed from April 5, so the specific day is unknown.

Erika with baby Ilze in front of a bombed out building 1945

January 7, 1946

(Nikolajs) It came to be that there was no time to write and now, more than half a year later, I haven't written a single line. Things have been up and down during this time and I will try to briefly describe them.

We didn't live in Wuppertal long after the American occupation, because we were constantly threatened by the Russians. They would come and steal the boxes left behind by those who went to Bairotra and generally tried to make our lives uncertain. Our camp leadership with Skalders at the head did a lot to help us get out of this unpleasant place. That finally succeeded and we were accommodated at the Polish camp in Bonn-Duisdorf. Here everything went as if on a thread[112] - the Polish komandant presented to the Latvian men, already the next day, to drive to France together with the Polish men and

---

[112] Idiomatic expression apparently indicating great efficiency.

enter the American army's paramilitary service guarding prisoners. The issue was decided that the Polish would protect us from being sent to the "roginu"[113] and all the Latvian men, in gratefulness for that, would have to enter the American paramilitary service. The next day in the evening we already found ourselves together with the Poles on a train on the way to France. We rode through beautiful Belgium and almost all the time along the Meuse River. Really wonderful scenery all around! We spent about half a day in the Belgian city of Namur. The city was hopping and almost everything a heart could desire was available to be bought in stores. Among other things, magnificent beverages, cakes, pastries, fruit, berries.[114]

* * *

---

[113] Not sure of spelling or translation.

[114] End of the diary. With Nikolajs riding the train through the Belgian countryside, one can only imagine what Erika and baby Ilze were going through back in the camp.

Chapter V - After the Diary - The Continuing Story

Not much is known of the years the little family of three spent in Germany immediately following the end of the diary.

Erika, Nikolajs and baby Ilze ca. 1946

They must have moved again, since I do remember many references to a place called Greven, a city located near Hamburg. Over the years, my parents referred to many of the places they had lived in Germany, including Wuppertal, Esslingen and Schwelm, where Ilze was born.

Erika and Nikolajs frolicking agaist the backdrop of a bombed-out building, Germany ca. 1945

In 1946, Germany was divided as shown in the following map. Dagnija Leimane describes in detail the differences between the American zone, where food was plentiful and DPs were well cared for, and the other zones, in particular, the British, where food and care were scarce.

Map of Germany 1946
www.history.army.mil

Other than while they were traveling, Erika and Nikolajs spent all of their time in Germany within the British zone. With so much of their journey not recorded, it is difficult to ascertain exactly where they lived in the years between the end of the journal and their arrival in England (ca. 1949).

According to Nikolajs and Erika's references, a substantial amount of time must have been spent in Greven, a location with a significant Latvian population, as evidenced by the existence of a newspaper entitled "Trimda", or "Exile".

I remember conversations between my parents in which they mentioned having been in Esslingen, a place I later discovered had a Latvian population of over 5,000 (Neimane, 2016).

Latvian newspaper "Exile"

---

115 www.archive.org.lv

A picture book inscribed to "Garenu 1947 trimdā" that may have been a gift from another Latvian in the camp.

A photo of Greven in 1946 shows barracks that may have been of the type inhabited by Erika, Nikolajs and baby Ilze.

116

Greven 1946

I know Nikolajs, Erika and Ilze left Germany sometime in 1948 or 1949, but no details are available and I only
know they ended up in England. I was born on September 15,
1951 in Paddington Hospital, London. At the time and, as recorded on my birth certificate, we lived at 1 Princess Road,
Willesden. In researching the location now, it appears that
Princess Road is now located in an area called Kilburn Park. I
have early memories of being wheeled in a stroller along a

---

116 www.archive.org.lv

shop-lined street that may have looked something like this un-dated photo of Willesden Green. I remember being in the bak-ery in my stroller and being given a pastry in a small, brown paper bag by the baker.

Willesden Green

I believe we lived upstairs and I do remember being carried up a darkened stairway. Over the years, my young memory was augmented by my mother's recounting of wheel-ing me in my stroller into the baker, the green grocer and the

---

[117] www.flickr.com

butcher in this same neighborhood. This was probably a daily event to secure groceries for the family.

Without anyone to confirm our exact locations, I can only go by what is listed in documents. We must have moved at least one more time to another address in London - 57 Constantine Road – since this is the address listed on my father's ticket to sail to Canada.

Real estate on Constantine Road is expensive today, so our little apartment at number 57 is now part of an exclusive neighborhood. Now, so many decades later and with memories faded, I am not sure if my shop-lined street was in Willesden, or Golders Green, about which I kept hearing as a child, or Constantine Road in Hampstead.

The last few months were spent at 124 Powys Lane in Palmers Green, the address listed on a letter from the Canadian Pacific Railway to my mother dated 4 April 1955. This must have been the address of my godparents, Lauma and Alberts Jerums. Erika, Ilze and I stayed with them from the time Nikolajs left England in December, 1954 until we left in May, 1955.

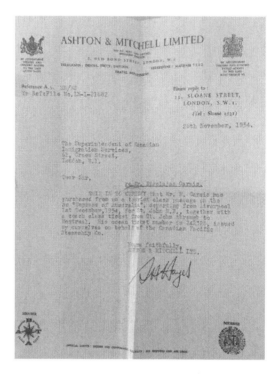

Ticket for Nikolajs' ship's passage to Canada

My godfather, Alberts Jerums, was a well-known Latvian conductor and my godmother, Lauma, was his wife. Their daughter, Jana, became the very first Latvian Lutheran female minister. I had brief contact with her on social media in 2014.

Ilze, Jana Jerums, Ingrid age 3, Spring 1955 London

According to reports from my parents, I was a cheerful child, as the following photo from the fall of 1954 seems to show. This must have been taken shortly before Nikolajs' departure for Canada. Although most photographs show me smiling, I remember feeling not so cheerful, even at a young age. One particular incident involves Ilze and Jana Jerums, a minor situation in which Ilze defended Jana and reprimanded me, even though I was not at fault.

Ingrid age 3 ca. late 1954

* * *

Chapter VI - Canada, the Early Years

In December of 1954, Nikolajs departed England for Canada to lay the groundwork for moving all of us there once he found a job and a place to live. In the meantime, Erika, Ilze and I would live with my godparents, Lauma and Alberts Jerums in their beautiful English Tudor style home. I still remember the "tower room" filled with sunshine and the nearby park with swans in the lake.

Erika, Ilze and I left London in early May, 1955, traveling to Liverpool by train, then boarding the Empress of Australia on May 13 to sail across the Atlantic to Canada. The Empress of Australia was the last wooden hulled ship to sail the Atlantic and it was scuttled not long after our trip.

Since arriving in December, Nikolajs had begun to establish a life in Montreal. I was too little to know much of the reality of what it took for Erika and Nikolajs to move to yet another country, but it was, no doubt, as frightening and daunting as the previous moves to Germany and England.

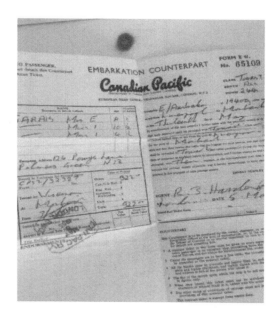

Our ticket to Canada on the Empress of Australia[118]

---

[118] The ticket lists my age as 4, although I was only three at the time.

The Empress of Australia – photographer unknown.

The journey on the Empress of Australia took five days and, though I was only three, I have a few distinct memories of life as a ship's passenger. Erika and Ilze experienced a great deal of seasickness in the stormy Atlantic seas, but I seemed to have no trouble staying upright and feeling well while they swayed in the passageways, stopping occasionally at the standing ashtrays to retch. Both of them spent time in their berths moaning – I must have sat and watched, for what would a three-year old do by herself on an ocean liner? I remember sitting at a table in the lavish dining room, with white tablecloths and silverware, tasting grapefruit for the first time in my short life. Chairs and tables were bolted to the floor and boiled eggs were served in silver egg cups. For some reason, I can remember only breakfast.

The weather finally cleared as we entered the St. Lawrence River after five days of travel. I remember the sun shining on the water as we sailed toward our destination. We landed in Montreal on May 17 where we were reunited with husband and father. The reunion must have been emotional for Erika and Nikolajs having been separated for several months.

The man on the right in the following photograph is Boris Godins, a close family friend who came to pick us up in the port of Montreal. The photograph was taken by another close family friend, Reinhards Simanis, who took thousands of photos and 8 millimeter film throughout my childhood. Both are deceased, but both played important roles in our lives, beginning with this incredible reunion.

Ingrid, Nikolajs, Ilze, Erika, family friend Boris Godins

On arrival, we lived in a rented two-bedroom apartment on Grand Boulevard in the Notre Dame de Grace (NDG) neighborhood of Montreal's west side. Of all the places I have lived, NDG is probably the closest to what I would call home and, although I am no longer interested in living there, I remember it in detail. At the time, milk was delivered by a milkman with a horse and cart. Streetcars ran up

113

and down Grand Boulevard and I played with neighbor children in the yard surrounding the apartment buildings.

Summers included many family activities and, even though we were probably rather poor according to today's standards, we always spent at least a week on vacation. My earliest memories are of staying on a working farm for a week, unfortunately clear in my mind because of a fire in one of the adjacent cabins. I can remember standing around the next morning as the pungent smell pervaded the air and adults commiserated about the loss.

Other vacations took us to rivers and lakes not far from Montreal, sometimes staying with friends who would rent out rooms in their houses in the country. One of my clearest and saddest memories is of a Sunday night when Nikolajs was preparing to return to the city for the workweek while we stayed in the country. I couldn't help but cry when he left and now I can feel the sadness I felt then as I think of him.

The family on vacation in the summer of 1957

Another of my more vivid childhood memories is of my mother walking me to my first day at Willingdon School on September 8, 1957. It was rainy and I wore a sparkling new, white vinyl raincoat and hat. My school life began with first grade, robbing me of the opportunity to attend kindergarten. It had been determined that, with my birthday in September, I was too young the previous year when I would turn 5, but in this next year I was already reading and writing, so too advanced for kindergarten. I remember Erika as being happy during that walk to school, whether because school held good memories for her, or she was just glad to be getting rid of me. At the time, my sister, Ilze, was also attending the same school, but in grade seven.

Ilze, Erika, Ingrid on 5ᵗʰ birthday, Nikolajs

Many experiences flood back in recalling life on Grand Boulevard. I had friends in the apartment buildings with whom I made "mudpies" and ran around all summer. My mother worked only part-time during these years and, although money was clearly scarce and my parents would probably remember things differently, I don't remember lacking for anything. For a time, Erika ran a special sewing machine at home as she took in torn stockings to repair. I remember not being able to sleep having to listen to the incessant hum of the sewing machine late into the night. Eventually I was able to help my mother with the stockings, pulling out snags by hand with a needle.

Nikolajs and Erika in Grand Blvd. apartment ca. 1957

Many other memories exist of the small apartment on Grand Boulevard. Nikolajs and Erika socialized often, celebrating birthdays, the Latvian tradition of names' days, and holidays with elaborate buffets and luscious baked goods. We had a large radio in the kitchen and I remember music and programs playing while Erika cooked. Some of the meals were simple, such as macaroni with bacon, but we always ate well.

Winters were severe, with much snow as is typical in Montreal. However, the only time school was ever cancelled was during an ice storm in 1959. The power was out, so Ilze and I started walking to school as always, this time stepping over downed wires and treading carefully on the icy sidewalks. Finally, someone shouted to us that school was closed and we returned home to our dark apartment.

Once Ilze was in high school, she and I moved into the larger bedroom so she could have room for a desk to study. I missed the coziness of the smaller bedroom off the kitchen where we had been. I used to wake up early on Sunday mornings and read the Saturday newspaper, beginning with the comics that I still enjoy reading today.

* * *

Chapter VII - Life Changes

In 1961 we moved to a first-floor duplex eight blocks away from the apartment. It was one of four units in the older building, a luxurious abode compared to the apartment on Grand Blvd. Ilze and I now each had our own room, and we had a basement where I could play out my fantasy of being a teacher. The apartment had a 54-foot hallway with doors at each end and, to this day, I can still conjure up unpleasant memories of seeing a face reflected in one of the doors. My tiny bedroom off the kitchen was my sanctuary. The window overlooked an old garage roof and our clothesline, but at least I didn't have to share the space with Ilze.

I continued to attend Willingdon school even into my first year of high school, when I should have attended West Hill High School a block away. The high school building had become over-crowded and the eighth grades had to be housed in spare classrooms at Willingdon. This was, at times, difficult and confusing for the new eighth graders, who felt isolated from the main high school.

119

I became close friends with a Latvian girl whose parents knew mine. Coincidentally, my father knew her mother from playing volleyball in Latvia and her father had been in my mother's fifth grade class in school (see photo, p. 14). She lived on the next street, so just about every day after school we hung out at her house and smoked stolen cigarettes in her father's garage.

Life continued to become more complicated for my family as Ilze's mental health began to deteriorate while I headed into my teenage years. My father was working for a company right down the street, so he was able to come home for lunch every day. Erika was working for an accountant across the city. Ilze began to hear voices. She would invite me into her room to listen to the radio announcer "speaking directly to" her. What could I say? My attempts to alert my parents to her strange behavior must have been ignored, since she kept getting worse and no one seemed to be doing anything about it.

In April of 1967, my parents bought a house in the suburb of Greenfield Park south of Montreal and quite a distance away from my school and my friends. It had long been a dream of theirs to own a house so they could keep up with their friends and provide a suitable environment for the family. The repercussions of this move are still felt today in the memories I carry with me.

Erika and Nikolajs in front of the new house 1967

The Greenfield Park house was a newly constructed raised ranch located at the end of a street lined with apartment buildings and an elementary school. Behind us was a huge field that eventually became one in a series of many shopping centers on a busy thoroughfare. Nikolajs loved the yard, filling it with beautiful plantings and a fruit and vegetable garden.

The backyard was the scene of many social events, including the after-party to my first wedding, and also for hours of lying in the sun to achieve the perfect tan. Access to the city was achievable by bus and subway, so life continued as before....or so Nick and Erika thought.

My life had been thoroughly disrupted by this move to the suburbs. I was granted permission by school board officials to continue attending the same high school in NDG, but it would require a car ride each day with my father followed by a bus ride for total travel time of about an hour. This meant my participation in after school activities or even early morning pre-school hanging out would be curtailed, seriously affecting my already tenuous social connections caused by my deep shyness. After a while, I stopped using the required traveling as an excuse and became creative in how I was able to find my way home using public transportation or even hitchhiking. However, the damage had been done and I began to suffer feelings of isolation.

The family 1967

Meanwhile, Ilze's mental state deteriorated rapidly as, we later found out, it was fueled by prescriptions for diet pills by our family doctor. In subsequent years, I found out he was fondly referred to by patients as the "pill doctor". Ilze was hospitalized not long after we moved into the house in April of 1967 and I have vivid memories of the day she came home from the hospital. We were walking along a neighborhood street and, in the exact words, stated,

"This is all your fault." I have carried this around ever since, never truly accepting why her illness (paranoid schizophrenia) drove her to blame me for her condition. I understand her jealousy and why she regarded me as the intruder into her relationship with my father, but acceptance of these facts was difficult for me. I'm sure doctors attempted to medicate her and, in later years, I learned that Ilze had been given shock treatments. However, the patterns of behavior that had started in her teen years continued along with her increasingly vehement denials that anything was wrong. Although our relationship did undergo periods of improvement, the notion of blame never completely dissipated.

Nikolajs tried his best to ignore her illness, but Ilze developed deep resentment toward him, according to her, the result of his treatment of a certain love interest of hers. Years later, when Nikolajs' health was declining rapidly due to metastasized prostate and kidney cancer, Ilze still treated him as if he had wronged her deeply, while he had only ever loved his firstborn daughter. Nikolajs was not always very good at expressing his emotions, so Ilze never quite believed his deep love for her. Her insecurity caused her to focus on the negative interactions between them instead of the underlying emotions.

Erika would struggle with her own demons later in life, reaching a point where she, too, heard voices and imagined transgressions against her where none existed. Although she loved Ilze very much, Erika was unequipped to handle her older daughter and insisted we only needed to be nice to her. I don't remember too much of my mother's reactions to Ilze's behavior other than to admonish me that I should be kind to her. As was my passive habit, I agreed that I would, but often did not. I was angry with Ilze for being sick, and angry with my parents for not doing anything to force her to take her medication or get treatment. I especially did not accept that I was at fault for any of it. I had no answers, but it was not right and these feelings never changed.

* * *

Rexy, the family dog with Erika, 1987

Chapter VIII - Erika in Later Years

Erika returned to Latvia for a brief trip in 1987. No doubt, it left her with mixed emotions, but at least she had the opportunity to visit with her sister, Erna, and many cousins and extended family members.

Erika with her niece, Ruta, and Ruta's daughter, Laura.

Nikolajs' nephew Andrejs, sister Erna, Erika, unknown male during Erika's visit to Latvia in 1987.

During a visit to the United States in 2007, Erna's daughter, Ruta, was able to provide information about the family, especially my fascinating grandmother, Liza. Ruta often recalled her brief meeting with Erika in 1987, noting how different I had turned out from what she expected after hearing what my mother said about me. Apparently, Erika portrayed me as ladylike, well-mannered and altogether different from the casual, easygoing individual Ruta was visiting. This discrepancy in observations underscored how little Erika really knew me and how her perception of me was more like the person she expected me to be than who I really was.

Erika often seemed to carry a burden of misery that she was quick to use to make us all feel guilty…for something. Now, after reading and translating her perceptions in 1944, her bitterness was understandable, though her resulting behavior may not have been completely justified. The enthusiasm for life that showed even during the DP camp days could not survive the difficult years in England, nor the voyage to yet another strange country. The playful relationship she may have craved with Nikolajs was tarnished by daily life and the love between them was fragile until the end of Erika's life.

I can see now that Erika's bitterness had a clear basis in her experiences during the war and I understand why she never seemed completely happy. Although she and my father ended up living together and ostensibly loving each other for almost 50 years, I'm not sure, even after all that time, that he was the true love she hoped for. She was young when life tore her away from her beloved home and family, probably immature as youngest children sometimes are, and so unsure of her future. Whatever coping skills she would have needed to deal with the horrors of war and its aftermath were most likely undeveloped and her ability to rise above her own misery was impeded by circumstances beyond her control.

In 1968, Erika developed breast cancer, in those days a somewhat misunderstood ailment that she and Nikolajs strove to keep quiet from family and friends. Some people may have shunned her, thinking cancer was somehow contagious. Erika had surgery to remove her left breast and several lymph nodes. This was followed by harsh radiation treatments that I remember left her skin burned and dark. I remember visiting her in the hospital and feeling somewhat confused about the true nature of her illness. She recovered from that first bout with cancer and, after three months of recuperation, went back to work at her job in a large financial organization. On her return, her colleagues presented her with a lovely Easter cactus that I have been propagating ever since into generations of plants that bloom each winter.

Erika continued to work until retirement age, filling her spare time with knitting and reading. She enjoyed walking the dog and cross-country skiing in the winter. Since I moved away from Montreal in 1973, I saw her only once every year or two for the rest of her life. We wrote letters and talked on the phone about once a month, but it was not until my own children grew up and moved away that I realized the depth of how much she must have missed me.

Erika loved her grandsons (my children), although she often disagreed with my life choices and their upbringing, that was so different from her own. Ever the socialite, Erika along with Nikolajs participated in Latvian society as well as frequent get-togethers with their circle of friends.

Nikolajs, Erika, Eric, Ingrid, Peter, October 1991

Church was more of a social event than a regular part of her daily life, but Erika's faith seemed to grow toward the end of her life. No doubt, this helped her through the miserable final years of her difficult existence. Her breast cancer returned with a vengeance along with ovarian cancer and she died in June of 1992 at age 70. I saw her in her hospital room two days before her death and we were able to tell each other, "I love you".

* * *

Chapter IX – Nikolajs in Later Years

Nikolajs never returned to his beloved homeland. His family tree has been hard to trace. Nikolajs never appeared to want to talk about his relatives, either that, or he simply could not remember much about his family. Any information I do have about his family outside of my own memories was provided by my cousin, Ruta.

Nikolajs had a great sense of humor and, as he aged, he loved to laugh and tell jokes. He enjoyed watching shows such as "Benny Hill" and "The Carol Burnett Show", often laughing to the point of tears at the antics of the comedians. He entertained us at the dinner table when we would visit and, in spite of disapproving looks from Erika, loved to show his humorous side to Peter and Eric. They still talk of his trompe l'oeil tricks like taking off their noses.

Nikolajs would have loved to spend more time with his grandsons, but it was difficult for us to make the trip from Connecticut to Montreal more than once or twice a year. He and Erika did visit us on several occasions and, on those trips, he was able to participate in activities such as salt-water fishing and boating that he otherwise may never have experienced. Nikolajs enjoyed my husband, Dan's, company and for years he spoke of the huge bluefish they caught on their excursions into Long Island Sound. Unfortunately, both Nikolajs and Erika died before Dan and I bought our first house, but we often felt they visited us as angels as our lives continued to improve.

Nikolajs' nephew, Andrejs, went to Canada for a visit in the eighties, but contact with him was lost when my parents died. According to letters from Andrejs in 1972 and 1973, a new owner was in possession of the house on Džutes street, but he still lived in it and could not be thrown out. Nevertheless, he was concerned about his future, seeming to want Nikolajs to intervene somehow and possibly lend him money. Apparently, Andrejs was employed as a teacher, but half of his salary went to support his children, so he must have been divorced at this point.

Nikolajs and Andrejs in Montreal in the 1980s

Nikolajs was a commercial artist by profession, working for companies to develop advertising layouts and packaging. At home, he sketched in charcoal and painted in oils. Today many examples of his work grace the walls in our home, and I am grateful for this precious legacy.

A sketch of Ingrid, age 3, by Nikolajs

A feeble effort was made to teach me how to paint in oils, but I lacked confidence and Nikolajs lacked to ability to let go of my hand long enough to allow me to develop my own talents, so I never pursued the avocation. He did occasionally "help" me with school projects, although I remember being almost embarrassed that whatever he did seemed more professional than it should have if done by a child.

Nikolajs' painting of Old Sailors' Church in Montreal, Erika on right

Nikolajs was a loving father. He and I spent a great deal of time together, from grocery shopping on Friday evenings to fishing, to Sunday morning walks on Montreal's Mount Royal. Although I was not encouraged to play any, I shared his love of athletics and we would spend time watching hockey and other sports on television.

Eventually I learned to play a little tennis and cross-country ski, both of which we did together. I was never the athlete he probably hoped for, but we shared animated discussions debating the strengths and weaknesses of Montreal Canadiens players and Olympic athletes.

Nikolajs was a very generous person. His desire to please the three women in his family by providing them with the very best food, clothing, and social life led to financial difficulties that were only uncovered in later years. Erika had to assume control of their fiscal affairs in order to avoid complete collapse. Nikolajs' need to fulfill our material wishes no doubt stemmed in part from the deprivation of the early years.

Nikolajs in his garden 1991

The last part of Nikolajs' life must have been very sad for him and I regret not making more time to visit. Erika died in 1992, so, for almost two years, he was alone with Ilze, whose mental illness made it difficult for her to function and communicate normally. To her, he was a burden, especially with his increasing need for personal care.

Nikolajs had apparently been ill with cancer for many years, but his general health was so good, he was able to outlive Erika and exist until May 1994 when the cancer metastasized from his prostate and kidneys into his brain. I remember his friendly nature changing during those last few years into angry outbursts, no doubt caused by the mounting illness. I visited him in the hospital a few days before his death and, much as I was able to with Erika, we exchanged "I love you" as parting words.

A few of the paintings we have in our home are dated 1994, so, as late as a few months before his death, Nikolajs continued to practice his beloved art of oil painting. His generous spirit continues to influence our lives and, now that we are settled in Florida, we still wish he were here to enjoy the warmth and relaxed lifestyle.

* * *

Chapter X - Ilze

Little Ilze never seemed to shed the effects of having been born surrounded by falling bombs and lacking good nutrition due to the scarcity of food. The major life changes in moving from Germany to England and then to Canada, no doubt, also affected her fragile psyche. She was a doting older sister most of the time, at least while I was young.

Ilze with me on my fourth birthday, September 15, 1955

Although she was extremely intelligent and went on to become a talented violinist, as a teenager, Ilze was diagnosed with paranoid schizophrenia, a mental illness caused by chemical imbalance. Her behavior toward all of us changed drastically as her illness progressed. These days she would probably also be labeled as bipolar, manic depressive as well as paranoid schizophrenic and psychotic. Her pride and my parents' codependency stood in the way of proper treatment, so she drifted in and out of bouts of depression, mania, and delusion.

Ilze on her confirmation day, May 1962

Ingrid and Ilze, 1994

I have lost touch with Ilze since the last time we spoke on the phone sometime in 2004. The last I knew, she was living in our old neighborhood of NDG in Montreal, but she struggled with reality and it is possible that she ended up in some sort of public facility. I can only imagine what may have befallen her in the harsh world of a city in which she maintained no connections and sought no help. I am asked why I don't make an effort to find her, but so many years have passed since I had any information of her whereabouts, I wouldn't know where to start to try and find her in a city of two million where the first language is French. I pray for her safety.

*   *   *

Chapter XI - My Cultural Inheritance

This brief chronicle contains vivid description of the lives of two young refugees from a small country whose citizens have withstood centuries of conflict. Nikolajs and Erika may not have appreciated their heritage in their youth as much as they would later in life, exiled from their homeland. As a result of living in a country that was almost always occupied, Latvians often have a deep sense of ethnic and cultural pride, which I inherited, especially from my father. I am still proud to mention my Latvian heritage whenever the occasion arises.

Growing up, our family participated in social and cultural activities based in our Latvian language and traditions. Our church was Latvian and, though we attended primarily on significant occasions such as Christmas and Easter, many other events took place on church property. Each Christmas, we attended the "eglite", or Christmas party in the church basement. This photograph was taken at the first one I attended in Montreal as a four-year-old in December 1955. Some of the other children pictured have remained lifelong friends.

Ingrid is in the third row, second from right – December 1955

Our church owned property in the countryside and many summer weekends were spent eating, drinking, singing and dancing in Tervete. The property encompassed fields along the fast-moving Rouge River about 85 miles north of Montreal. This next photo captures the group of churchgoers singing (perhaps the Latvian national anthem "Dievs Svēti Latviju) in the early years of Tervete's existence. Many other activities took place, including celebrations of midsummer and June 24, "Jāņi", or "John Day".

Ingrid to right of girl with two flags, Erika with large purse

A children's summer camp was established at Tervete in 1965 that still operates today. Children with Latvian roots attend and participate in activities common to summer camp, but also designed to immerse them in Latvian culture.

Another important institution in the lives of Montreal's Latvians was Latvian School. Most Latvian children in Montreal attended every Saturday morning throughout their elementary and high school years, through grade ten. For some unexplained reason, whether it was the difficulty of transporting me across town every week, or the fact that I spoke Latvian reasonably well, I was not sent to Latvian School. Finally, since all my friends attended and, because I wanted to participate in folk dancing, I was allowed to go in tenth grade, where I graduated with all those who had gone all along. In addition to dancing at the School, some of us also joined the official Montreal folk dance group, Ačkups. The group consisted of about twenty dancers ranging in ages 15 through 25.

The 1966-67 season of folk dancing practices once or twice a week and performances at some of the more prominent Latvian cultural events was in preparation for the 1967 World's Fair in Montreal, known as Expo '67. I still have the miniature flag and the Latvian Power button most of us wore as we roamed the spectacular grounds in our folk costumes.

Buttons from 1967 and 1968

That year (1967), because the Soviets were in attendance, we, the expatriate Latvians, were forced to perform off the official Expo '67 fairgrounds. When a group of us tried to wave our Latvian flags inside the Soviet pavillion during a performance of Russian dancers, some large, burly Russians promptly escorted us out of the building. The following year, as most of the pavillions remained and the fairgrounds bustled with another year of international events, we were "allowed" to perform on the official grounds. The following photograph shows me in costume at the 1968 Baltic Day celebration on the Expo grounds.

At the Baltic Day celebration, Expo 1968

I continued to folk dance until I got married in 1973 to a Latvian boy I had met at a national Latvian Song Festival[119] in Cleveland in 1968. These festivals include participation of choirs and folk dance groups from all over the world. A few years later, while we were living in the Boston area, we both danced in the local Latvian folk dance group and the two of us performed a solo in Boston Garden during another Song Festival. Although we divorced in 1982, he and I continued a friendship that benefited our sons in later life.

In the late 60s, I was a member of a Latvian sorority. Fraternities and sororities were highly regarded in Latvia as pinnacles of society and, though not quite as important outside Latvia, still engaged many college graduates throughout the world. Our group of "sisters" met on a regular basis, learning, discussing, singing, and socializing in much the same way that similar groups of educated women were doing across the country to maintain Latvian university traditions. My parents encouraged me to belong, especially since any chance they would

---

[119] These festivals began in Latvia in 1873 and continue to be held in Latvia. They are also held every 4 years (most recently in San Diego in September 2015) in the United States/Canada and are attended by thousands of Latvians. Dancers perform traditional folk dances and choirs and other musical groups sing various types of Latvian music, all in celebration of Latvian culture.

have had to attend university or be in a fraternity or sorority was lost because of the war. Marriage and moving separated me from that life and I lost touch with all but a few of my sorority sisters.

Over the years, most of the connections I had in my youth were not maintained, but I am proud of my Latvian heritage and eagerly speak of it whenever I have the opportunity. Visits from my cousin, Ruta's, daughters in the past two years have afforded me the chance to speak Latvian and even to meet a couple of Latvians here in Florida. My sons are also proud of their Latvian origin and, although they don't speak much of the language, they enjoy some of the traditions they learned as children.

* * *

Chapter XII - Full Circle

Life continued for the Garais family as we coped individually with Ilze's mental illness, Erika's cancer, and my painful isolation from the childhood neighborhood where my friends still lived. I can only imagine what Nikolajs was going through while the women in his life struggled with their various problems. I survived an episode of particularly severe depression in the early 70s and, in the summer of 1973, married a young Latvian with whom I had only a brief history as a way to escape the difficulties of living with my family.

My new husband and I moved to Fort Jackson, South Carolina immediately after the wedding to take up residence where he was stationed in the US Army. Of course, this was quite a culture shock for me and, along with my complete lack of understanding of what marriage was supposed to entail, served as the shaky beginning of the nine years we would spend together. Not only did I have to figure out how to be a good wife on a personal level, I also had to assume to role of Second Lieutenant's wife within the structured and demanding society of the military. I vacillated between enjoying the formality of the chain of command and wanting to rebel against always being told exactly what to do and how to do it. The contrast no doubt originated in my relationship with Erika, who would have loved the Officers' Wives functions and formal balls, but whose partialities I would have defied, at least in my mind.

After two years at Fort Jackson, my husband received orders for Germany. We were excited about the prospect of moving to Europe, but I was just as blind to the scope of this event as I had been to my sudden wedding and relocation to a life in the American south. As I reread this now, I realize that my life and its many moves somewhat mirror the changes Erika had to endure as she moved from one country to another, though definitely not the crisis of war.

Perhaps it was the result of having heard my parents speaking German, or the similarities in food products, or maybe the presence of guiding spirits, but I felt more at home in Germany than I had in Canada or the United States. We traveled throughout the country, visiting Wuppertal, where my parents spent time in the DP camps and Schwelm, where Ilze was born, among other places. We could only imagine the life my parents had to lead back then, although we did see un-touched ruins in the city that were likely there when they went to find ice cream.

On April 14, 1977, our twin sons were born, so they are part of the legacy and the German connection. The story continues even later to the day they celebrated their seven-teenth birthday. On that day, 54 choir members from their high school, along with 5 teachers and 7 parents, left on a singing tour of Germany and Austria. Had the boys been 18, they would have risked being drafted into the German military, since they possess German birth certificates as well as US born abroad. As it was, Peter and Eric got to see some of the land in which they were born, experience the culture, and even taste the beer that flows so readily.

Shortly after the boys were born, we returned stateside, a motley collection of luggage, pets, and two very young babies who, fortunately, tolerated the long flight fairly well. My par-ents came to meet us at the airport in New York and drove us back to Montreal where we spent a few weeks recovering from the experiences of the previous months. Although Erika had been shocked and somewhat displeased that we expanded our family, she was enamored of the little babies. Eventually we moved to Massachusetts where we lived with my in-laws for three months until we were able to find an apartment of our own.

Life went on, the boys grew and thrived, and we made efforts to go to Montreal at least once a year to visit my family. Nikolajs was lovingly accepting of anything in my life, while Erika seemed to work hard to find fault wherever possible. She criticized my husband and disparaged how we were raising our children, even suggesting they would be better off living with her and Nikolajs than with their own parents. I did my best to tolerate her disapproval, although I do remember some heated arguments on the subject.

A series of events led to the eventual deterioration of my marriage and I filed for divorce after learning of my husband's dalliance with a friend. We had been living in Connecticut for several years and were both working at the same manufacturing company. A mutual friend introduced me to Dan, whom I would marry soon after the divorce was final and with whom I celebrate thirty-five years together in May of 2017.

As much as Erika criticized my first husband, she was even less impressed with Dan. Even though she hadn't yet met

him, she disliked him enough to refuse to attend our small
wedding, and never really accepted him as a person or as my
husband. Fortunately, Nikolajs was his usual gracious, kind
self, learning to accept Dan and enjoying fishing and other activities in the brief time they spent together.

The greatest resistance to my new marriage came from
Ilze. Her pervasive dislike and fear of men caused her to treat
Dan with disrespect and disdain. During one visit to my family,
she lost control of her emotions to the point where Nikolajs
had to restrain her physically. Not wanting Peter and Eric to
be around this volatile behavior, we left to spend the rest of
our trip with a friend. Dan never returned to their home and
my parents died without seeing him again.

Many years later, happily married and still living in
Connecticut, Dan and I traveled to Italy and Austria, spending
a couple of days in Germany. Now all that is left is for me to
go to Latvia and the circle will finally be closed.

I miss my parents now. I regret not spending more
time with them while they were alive and I wish the diary had
surfaced when I could have asked the many questions I have
about their experiences. Although I was able to tell each of

them I loved them before they died, I will always feel that so many important thoughts were never shared. Erika and Niko-lajs did their best to raise me and I am grateful for their love.

Erika and Nikolajs, Christmas 1991

* * *

Chapter XIII - A Brief Conclusion

I hope you have enjoyed this glimpse into the lives of Erika and Nikolajs and the poignant details contained in the diary. My intention was to make public their experiences during the war and also to provide a context for the time span of the journal with particulars of our family life. The diary is one of very few possessions I have that belonged to my parents and is a treasure I intend to pass on to my sons to share the legacy with their children. This book has been a difficult journey for me, opening my eyes to the people my parents really were and offering some explanation for their behavior through their later years. I hope you enjoyed reading the book as much as I enjoyed writing it.

*   *   *

Acknowledgements

First of all, my thanks go to my parents for writing the diary and especially to my father for keeping it all those years. I'm sure his spirit can be felt in its pages as I feel him near me when I read it.

I am grateful to Debbie Lacouture for her willingness to read and reread the work, and for her insightful comments that helped me edit and add to the writing.

Most of all, thank you to my dear husband, Dan, for his everlasting encouragement. This never would have happened without you.

* * *

Bibliography

Dankers, Karlis. *DP – Memoir of a Postwar Childhood in Displaced Persons Camps in Germany*, Lulu.com, 2011

Neimane, Dagnija. *Flight From Latvia, A Six-Year Chronicle*, 2016

Sepetys, Ruta. *Between Shades of Grey*, Speak, 2012

About the Author

Ingrid McGowan is the youngest daughter of Nikolajs and Erika Garais, the subjects of this book. She attended various colleges and universities, most recently (2009) the University of Phoenix, earning a Doctorate of Management in Organizational Leadership. She has been married for 35 years to Danial, a native of Derby, Connecticut and a veteran of the United States Navy. Ingrid has forty-year-old twin sons, each of whom is married and has a son. Her retirement from 20 years in higher education in 2014 has allowed her to devote enough time to this book to prepare it for self-publishing. Other interests include golf, Mah Jongg, reading and teaching non-credit courses. She lives in Florida with her husband, Dan, and has already begun working on a second book.

Made in the USA
Lexington, KY
13 March 2019